# TRADITIONAL NORFOLK

(Just like his mother used to do)

by G.M. Dixon

Illustrated by Shelley Watson

Published by Minimax Books

ISBN 0 906791 21 3

© MINIMAX BOOKS LTD. 1982.
Deeping St. James, Peterborough.
All Rights Reserved. No part of this publication may be reproduced, stored in a retrieval system, or transmitted, in any form or by any means electronic, mechanical, photocopying, recording or otherwise, without the prior permission of the Copyright owner.

Printed in England

# CONTENTS

| | |
|---|---|
| Introduction | Page 4 |
| Breakfast | Page 6 |
| Soups | Page 7 |
| Fish | Page 10 |
| Pork | Page 14 |
| Poultry and Game | Page 16 |
| Beef | Page 20 |
| Lamb | Page 22 |
| Dumplings | Page 24 |
| Salads | Page 25 |
| Pickles | Page 28 |
| Puddings | Page 30 |
| Cakes and Buns | Page 35 |
| Drinks | Page 40 |

# Cooking in Norfolk

The traditions, lore and remedies of Norfolk are in some danger of being lost in these bustling, changing times. This little book has been compiled to place on record some of the cottage recipes and customs which people enjoyed years ago. In these days, when many wives are out to work, when the ease of convenience food is a real temptation, and when young housewives often live far from their mothers, the well-tried fare of traditional Norfolk is almost forgotten and seemingly redundant.

And yet young people are growing to realise more and more the value of good food and financial stresses are persuading the housewife more and more to economise with foodstuffs. There is also a growing interest in, and enthusiasm for, the things of the past, and the old recipes and foodstuffs are being revived and re-used. It is hoped that this collection will introduce you to some of the recipes used in Norfolk cottages in the past, and to those who know them it is hoped that they will provide a happy reminder.

The orchard, the vegetable plot, the pig at the bottom of the yard, the hens and the occasional fare from the fields provided most cottages with the food which they required. A visit to the village stores enabled the housewife to purchase what could not be grown, such as flour, sugar; tea, dried fruit and salt. Many foods, of course, were bottled, stored or dried.

Tending the garden and animals was the time-consuming preserve of the husband. But pleasant were the hours spent as he tended the garden, caring for the plants and animals there. He must have felt a real pride in the perfection of his produce as he bore it up the garden path towards the busy kitchen.

In the kitchen the housewife ruled supreme and the husband did not offer his services there for he knew that they would be proudly spurned. All the preparations for cooking were made upon the well-scrubbed kitchen table and all the day-to-day cooking was done on the kitchen range, blackened with Zebo every morning. These were awful things to light and they were very sensitive to draughts but the old housewives of the past worked culinary wonders with them. On the top were several plates which could be removed so that the heat would flow to the black saucepans which bubbled and frothed, containing puddings, stock, potatoes and vegetables. At the side of the fire was the small oven, heated by the fire, in which the pies for dinner or tea were baked. There was a little lever which controlled the flues, allowing the heat to circulate around the oven.

For the regulation baking day, usually a Friday, the housewife had to use the little wall oven, often built into the wall at the side of the range. Under the wall oven was a little firegrate and when this was lit the heat and smoke from the fire circulated around a contorted and intricate series of flues which were critical for an even temperature and an effective draught. Not many bricklayers remain who can construct one of these flues!

It would clearly be quite inappropriate to seek to regenerate these old types of ovens and cooking facilities, but just talk to people about the food of their young days in these old Norfolk cottages and a mouth-watering glow will suffuse their face as they speak.

Surely these old recipes should not be allowed to die, and it is to this end that this little book has been compiled. Described in the following pages are ordinary old-fashioned recipes with something for every occasion. I can assure you that if you bother you will make some really good food, with a taste that will make you cook more and more. All the recipes originate from this county. Maybe they are not unique to Norfolk and may, like many other good things, be shared by others; but surely this is but a testament to their value. They have not often been linked to any town or village, for this would have contrived a parochialism which really does not exist. The main thing is that they are genuine, truly Norfolk, with their origins in the past and their future in your hands!

May I sincerely wish you all success with them; and if at the first try they do not turn out, then have another try, for they are worth it.

G.M. Dixon,
June 1982.

**A good dinner sharpens the wit and**

**softens the heart.**

# Breakfast

Nothing warms a gentleman's heart more than a good breakfast. Certainly there are other arts and wiles that can please at other times but, first thing of a morning, with the sun shining clear from a wide Norfolk sky, or on a raw February morning, it is breakfast that will win his affections.

    Starters:    Orange juice, or grapefruit or cornflakes.

    Main course:    Two eggs and two large rashers of bacon, a sausage, fried bread, and fried tomatoes or mushrooms. Good English mustard and other condiments.

    Extras:    Toast, marmalade and lashings of butter, and, of course the teapot . . . not your modern coffee!

    As variations of the main course:
- Three scrambled eggs on toast.
- Two poached eggs on toast.
- A fat Yarmouth kipper
- Kedgeree.

After a breakfast like that, served with a smile and the local newspaper, the pressures of the world hold little fear. A man can walk tall on a beginning like that.

To clean a pine table

*If you are fortunate enough to own one of those lovely pine kitchen tables and it has properly been left unvarnished, then it will require the occasional scrub. Ladies of the past used one spoon of lime, two spoons of soap powder (detergent will do) and three spoons of silver sand. A little of this should be sprinkled on the table top and then well scrubbed in with a scrubbing brush. Afterwards rinse with clean water and dry.*

# Soups

You'll never go back to tinned soup if you once get a taste for these.

## PEA SOUP
A meal in itself.

> 1 large marrow bone cut and sawn up
> ½ lb split peas
> 1 carrot
> 1 onion
> 3–4 celery sticks.

Place the pieces of marrow bone in a large saucepan and well cover with water. Boil for some two to three hours. Leave this until the next day when the fat should be taken from the top, but leave the bones in. Add the split peas, and grate in the carrot, the onion and the celery. Boil for a further 3–4 hours. Take the bones out before serving.

To make a really good meal add a dumpling for each person (see page 24) twenty minutes before the meal.

Burgh, near Aylsham
*Mrs. Cushion, wife of a farmworker, stands outside her Norfolk red brick cottage with its russet tiles, while her photograph is taken by her son John. Later that year, for now it is April, 1914, he was to marry Helen from East Ruston. The intrepid camera shot over..."What did you want to take me in these old clothes for?" and "Well, thass how oi remember you." And then it was indoors for pea soup and dumplings before he cycled back to his work again.*

## ONION SOUP

    1 large marrow bone
    Rasher of lean bacon
    1 lb onions
    1½ oz cornflour
    Seasoning

Obtain the stock as for previous soups. Peel and thinly slice the onions and dust lightly with salt and pepper. Reheat the stock and add the onions when hot. Cut the rasher of bacon into small pieces and add with the onion. Bring to the boil and let it simmer for at least one-and-a-half hours. The longer it boils, the more flavour will be drawn out. Just before the meal add the cornflour, which has been mixed into a smooth paste with cold water, and stir gently.

For the best onion soup serve with either slices of fried bread or with a garnish of grated Cheddar cheese.

## KIDNEY SOUP

    ½ lb ox kidney
    1 large marrow bone
    1 small onion
    1 small carrot
    ½ turnip
    1 oz cornflour
    Seasoning

Saw or cut the marrow bone as for the pea soup and boil for two to three hours. Leave until next day and remove any fat as before. Remove all the fat from the kidney, wash, dry and cut into thin slices. Add to the stock and grate in the onion, carrot and turnip. Simmer for at least two hours. Add the cornflour mixed into a smooth paste with water and season to taste. Boil for a few minutes and then serve piping hot.

Flies in the house
*Near the back door of many unmodernised cottages a clump of mint is generally to be found. If you plant some mint in a kind of hanging basket and hang it near the window where it can get the sunshine, the flies will be kept away.*

## ASPARAGUS SOUP

Firstly we have to make some white stock

> 1 lb knuckle of veal
> 2 oz lean ham
> 1 small onion
> 1 stick of celery
> 7 peppercorns
> ½ teaspoon of salt.

Boil all of the above, with the vegetables grated, for two hours. Strain through a fine sieve and leave it for a day. Next day remove the fat.

Now, take and wash twelve asparagus tips and cut them into one inch lengths. Add them and 4 oz fresh green peas to the stock, together with a pinch of sugar and seasoning. Bring to the boil and let it simmer for about one hour.

To add a really delicious finish, after it has simmered for one hour remove from the stove and allow to cool a little. Add one gill of cream and stir this in gently. Replace on stove and bring to a gentle boil before serving piping hot.

Norfolk schoolboy
*Smart in his Norfolk jacket, breeches and patent leather boots... and oh, that handsome hat .... Hugh is just off back to the boarding school at Taverham, high class establishment for young gentlemen. 'Thank you for the buttonhole, mother; I will put it in a vase when I arrive .... coo, I liked that asparagus soup mother.'*

# Fish

## HOW TO DRESS A CROMER CRAB

Break off the claws and legs; crack them with the handle of a knife and remove the meat on to a small plate. Break off the apron which folds under the body at the rear.

Use a strong knife and force the shell open by wedging between the opening at the apron. Insert your thumbs at the opening between the shell halves, and pull upper shell away from the lower shell.

Alternatively, hold the crab in the left hand with the back towards you. Slip the fingers under the top shell and pull downwards to release it. Remove the spongy digestive tract which is still on the shell whilst holding it under running water. Hold the crab's body in your left hand and cut with a sharp knife the covering around the outer rim.

Remove the meat from the shell with a knife and mix with a little vinegar and salt and pepper to taste.

Replace in the shell, and then add the white meat on the top of it.

## SOUSED HERRINGS

Buy at least one herring for each person and clean them in the usual way. Place in a dish with a few peppercorns. Barely cover with vinegar, or vinegar and water if you don't like vinegar too much. Cook in an oven at 350° for half-an-hour.

*Stinging nettles*
*Marvellous plants, always to be found where man has lived. Lovely tea, which induces sleep, can be made from dried nettles. Nettle beds are also the breeding territory of some of our rarest butterflies. However, a bounding youngster who comes into contact with these on a picnic can disturb our ears with his yell. Dock leaves, always to be found near, applied to the affected part, will soon soothe the pain of the stings and restore the peace of the countryside.*

**Cromer**
"*We're here on holiday in 1908, and this little town of Cromer is a really delightful spot. Down here for the air, you know. Lovely fresh sea air, so healthy. So interesting too. Especially the time when the crab boats come in . . . those great strong men landing their sailing boats with deft strokes of the oars. Baskets of lovely crabs . . . we are to have one for tea in the hotel . . . the Metropole . . . this evening.*"

## KEDGEREE

A beautifully light dish to tempt even the most flagging of appetites. You need

    2½ oz rice
    1 egg
    ¼ lb flaked haddock
    1 hard boiled egg
    a scattering of peas
    seasoning

Wash the rice and boil it until tender and then tip it into a sieve and wash it through with cold water. Drain well and then add the cooked flaked haddock. Add a little pepper and salt and a beaten egg to bind the mixture. The mixture should then be placed into a double saucepan and reheated gently. Place in a dish and decorate the kedgeree with the sliced cold hard boiled eggs and add a scattering of peas just for colour. It can be served hot or cold—hot it is especially lovely.

## STOOKEY BLUES

## BLOATERS AND KIPPERS

Bloaters are herrings which have been lightly salted and smoked and Great Yarmouth is famed for their production.

Bloaters should be grilled to retain their flavour, although some people prefer them broiled.

To grill them, simply put the fish under a hot grill and when they are cooked lay them on a hot plate and rub a little butter into them. To broil them, split them open and remove the backbone, head, tail and fins. They should then be folded back double before being broiled for a little over five minutes.

A kipper was originally a salmon which had been split open and smoked, but the term has long been used to describe herring and other fish so treated. To really make them succulent, all that you have to do is to plunge them into boiling water for a minute or two to soften them. They should then be placed under a hot grill with a knob of butter laid upon them and a seasoning of black pepper. Absolutely delicious.

Having spent a Sunday afternoon at Stiffkey gathering the plentiful cockles at low tide you can drive home in your car with a half a bucketful of cockles and look forward to a glorious feast on Monday evening.

When you get home place the cockles in some fresh water and give them a good shake round before straining off the water. Cover the cockles with water again and on top of this add two or three handfuls of flour. They should then be left for the night. The cockles will then clean themselves of sand and at the same time take in some of the flour to make them fat and soft.

Next day place them into a large saucepan, after you have given them a good clean again. Just cover with some fresh water, and set them on a low heat. Every so often give them a shake up. When the shells open they are done and should be removed to cool. If you leave them in after the shells have been opened, they will turn hard and unpleasant.

Strain them through a sieve or a cloth. The cockles can then be picked out of their shells with a fork. A dash of vinegar and a little pepper and you have a feast fit for kings.

### Yarmouth Fishmarket
*Yarmouth fishmarket in its heyday, seen here just after the First World War, was a tremendously thriving industry. At the quayside nestled hundreds of fishing trawlers, their sail-furled masts a literal forest, their decks crowded with fishing nets and gear. On the quayside baskets and baskets of fish flowed out from the sheds . . . . and the fishermen themselves . . . . great characters as hard and humorous as the great North Sea they sailed. And for tea tonight . . . . lovely fresh herring . . . . scrumptious.*

# Pork

## PORK CHEESE

In other parts of the country it may be called brawn, but pork cheese rules in Norfolk. Simple to make and as delicious as it is simple.

Take a fresh hock from the butchers and boil it for at least two or three hours. By this time the meat will have left the bone and this tells you that it is cooked. Take the saucepan off the heat and remove all the pieces of bone. Add pepper and salt to taste and a grating of nutmeg, and then pour into a basin. It should be left in a cool place to set. Next day tip it out of the basin and a nourishing, delicious savoury is ready to serve.

*The pig at the bottom of the yard*
*"I don't know how we will ever manage to eat him. He has the scraps from the table and all the family come down to feed him. He fair loves it when we scratch his head, and grunts when we call his name. Mind you, they're some lovely hams . . . and we'll git some lovely pork cheese . . . chitterlings . . . and them sausages . . . my wad. Poor old boy . . . still, we'll git another one for next year."*

## PORK AND MARROW PIE

Certainly not one of your convenience foods but, once you have treated your family to this, they will always ask you for more. It has long been known that the lady who can cook one of these and smile afterwards will win my heart.

Ingredients

    1 lb of lean pork
    8 oz self-raising flour
    1/3 pint of water
    1 large onion
    6 oz suet
    1 medium marrow
    ¼ teaspoon salt

Cut the meat into small cubes and slice the onion. Lay these in a pie dish and cover with sliced marrow. Just cover with water and then with a piece of grease-proof paper or tinfoil. Pop it into an oven at 350°.

After two hours, remove it from the oven and allow to cool for thirty minutes.

Make the pastry from the other ingredients and, after the cooling period, place on the top of the meat and marrow. Return it to the oven and cook for a further thirty minutes at 350°–375°.

## PORK AND ONION DUMPLING

Again, delicious: on a winter dinner time it fills both the stomach and the heart with contentment.

Ingredients

    1 lb lean pork
    1 large onion
    8 oz flour
    4 oz suet
    A pinch of salt

Mix the suet, flour and salt into a pastry and roll out on the pastry board. Line the basin with pastry, leaving some over for the top.

Cut the pork up into very small cubes and slice the onion thinly. Place these in the lined basin and fill it three parts with water. Put in a little salt and pepper to taste. Cover with the rest of the pastry and it is now ready to cook. Either tie a pudding cloth over the basin or cover with greaseproof paper.

Place it into a saucepan which is half filled with water and cook for two to two-and-a-half hours.

Warts
*These curious and rather unattractive excrescences on the skin of the hands generally have cures that are well-based in folk lore. To those that are afflicted with them there is little relief. It has been said that the house-leek, or the inside of a broad bean pod, if rubbed upon them, will cure them. The most effective cure is the one that can be gained from the sale of them to a charmer who offers you a coin for them. Another way is to rub them with the skin of the potato and to bury this in the ground. When the potato skin rots, the warts will go.*

# Poultry

"Poultry of every species are sold, in the markets, ready picked and skewered fit for the spit; and are, in general, so well fatted, and dressed up in such neatness and delicacy, as shew the Norfolk housewives to be mistresses in the art of managing poultry."

from The Rural Economy of Norfolk, by Marshall published in London 1796.

## ROAST COCKEREL

Occasionally you will see a fresh farmyard cockerel for sale at a farmyard gate. Be careful not to get an old hen, past the age of laying eggs, for these are tough in the extreme. Sometimes you will be lucky enough to have had it killed, hung, plucked, and cleaned with the giblets, gizzard, liver, etc., in a little bag.

Take the cockerel and make sure that it has been well cleaned inside, and that the skin has been cleaned of all its feathers by singeing it. The legs should be cut off at the first joint, and the end of the bone cleaned. Lift each of the wings and make a small cut on the undersides of these; lay the gizzard under the left wing and the liver under the right. Truss by tying a piece of string to hold legs and wings.

Prepare a good rich stuffing by mixing together 3 oz breadcrumbs, 2 oz suet, a little chopped parsley, a beaten egg and salt and pepper to taste.

The chicken should be stuffed with this and afterwards the legs should be drawn up under the wings. A greased paper placed on the breast should keep it moist but the occasional basting helps. It should be roasted for 1-1½ hours and served with rich brown gravy and bread sauce.

## TURKEY CHEESE

This is a delicious way to use up that turkey which is always left over after Christmas and Easter.

Take a half-a-pound of cold turkey meat and two ounces of ham. The skin should be removed from the turkey and both ham and turkey chopped finely. Melt 1 oz of butter and stir in a teacupful of breadcrumbs, then add the meat, one ounce of cold stuffing and salt and pepper to taste. Then the whole mixture can be bound by mixing in one large egg, well beaten. Place the mixture in a well greased basin and steam for ¾ of an hour.

When it has cooled down a little it can be turned out on to a hot dish and given a good coating of cranberry jelly. Slices of fried bread served with the turkey cheese makes a delicious dish.

## ROAST WILD DUCK AND ORANGE SALAD

I once lived with an old lady who had a gamekeeper friend. Occasionally, after a day's shooting with his governor at Wroxham he would give her two lovely wild ducks. And, ohhh, the aroma! That delicious scent wafting from the kitchen on Saturday. Wild duck with piquant slices of orange. Mmmmmm.

First, make a friend of a gamekeeper. Then, get him to bring you two wild ducks. When he has gone, carefully draw the duck, singe and truss it and place it in a baking tin. Place a good lump of dripping on the breast and sprinkle well with flour. Roast it until it is a lovely golden brown and, as the old lady said, leave it on the underdone side.

Then comes the interesting piece. The old lady would then place it on a hot dish and remove the string. She would evenly place some water cress and slices of lemon on the hot duck. Then she would take the juice from the lemon, and from an orange, a sliced shallot, a gill of water and a glass of port. These would be mixed and poured over the duck. The hot dish would then be placed back in the oven until the liquid reached boiling point. It should boil for about five minutes.

It would then be strained, placed on a large platter and served with that orange salad. Fit for princes or . . . for you.

## CHRISTMAS GOOSE PIE

This is taken from a very old cookery book written in the fair hand of a housekeeper of a large house in North Norfolk.

Courage, girl . . .

Bone a large goose and a good fowl. Make a forcemeat of minced tongue, ham, veal and suet; season it with sweet herbs, parsley, lemon, pepper, mace and salt. Mix it with two eggs and fill the inside of the fowl with it; put the fowl inside the goose, make a gravy with the trimmings of the fowl, the tongue, any pieces that may be left of the veal, and a calf's foot or a cow's heel; stew the goose with the fowl inside, in this gravy for twenty minutes or half-an-hour. Then lay the goose in a dish, and place a piecrust over it; fill up any vacant spaces with slices of ham or the rest of the forcemeat. Strain the gravy through a jelly bag until it looks clear and pour it over the pie; lay some butter on the top and bake for three hours.

The old cook book then says: It is eaten cold, and if well made is extremely good and savoury; it will keep for a long time.

Sounds good doesn't it? Courage girl! Make one . . .
surprise him!!

# Game

## JUGGED HARE

The great brown hare of Norfolk eludes the legends of the county but passes into the folk lore through its inclusion in the traditional fare of the table. They are at the best for eating between September and late February.

The hare should be skinned, cleaned and jointed, and the joints wiped dry after washing. They should be dipped in flour and then lightly fried in butter so that the flavour may be retained during the jugging. When they have been very lightly browned, gravy or stock should be added and allowed to boil. After boiling both, the hare and the liquid should be poured into a large pie dish or earthenware jar. To the meat and gravy should be added a large sliced onion, pepper and salt and a glassful of port. The dish should then be placed into an oven and allowed to simmer for three to four hours at 350°.

After this time the dish should be taken from the oven and the meat placed on a large dish for serving. To the gravy can be added a further glass of port if it is a very cold day, and the gravy then re-heated gently. Served with redcurrant jelly, it provides a Saturday lunch of no mean standard.

## ROAST PHEASANT

The matter of hanging a pheasant until it has turned green is a delicate one and one worthy of discussion, but not in these pages.

When the pheasant are hung to your liking, pluck, clean and draw them. The tail feathers are worth saving for winter decoration, and some people use them to garnish the pheasant when it is cooked.

Pheasants can become awfully dry in the cooking and the secret lies in these little additions:

Stuff the drawn pheasant with a large shallot and some butter:

Before you place it in the oven wrap the breast with a nice thick fatty slice of bacon.

Cover well with either greaseproof or tinfoil and cook for three quarters to one hour in an oven at 350° according to the size of the bird. When cooked take the pheasant out, remove the bacon from the breast, shake some flour over the skin and then baste it before returning to the oven for five minutes to crisp.

Delicious with the traditional garnish of water-cress and eaten with fried potatoes, green beans or peas, bread sauce and thin gravy.

---

Selecting a dog to rear
*When the litter of puppies is about five or six weeks old bring them into your presence and suddenly stamp your foot. The one that does not run away, but holds up its tail, is the one to rear.*

# RABBIT PIE

Pies would seem to be traditional Norfolk fare and good stout meals they are for good stout men. Cooked on the kitchen range which was always burning merrily, they added a beautiful aroma to an already lovely home.

Joint the rabbit and put into a dish with a large sliced onion. Cover the meat and onion with water and cover with either tinfoil or greaseproof paper. Bake for 1½ hours in an oven at 350°.

After 1½ hours take the dish out of the oven and allow to cool for thirty minutes. Make a layer of pastry as for the pork and marrow pie and add this when the pie dish has cooled. Replace in the oven and cook for a further thirty minutes at 400°.

Uncle John's father from Burgh
*He loved his garden and his son John took this photograph near the apple trees at the bottom of the garden. Even though he worked on the land all the week, he still loved the wonder of the plants growing in the garden. Mind you, his jacket was just made with those large pockets in which you could lose a pheasant, partridge or rabbit. His wife's rabbit pie . . . words cannot describe the aroma . . . her recipe is here.*

# Beef

## BEEF STEW

Simple but rather nice.

A pound of shin beef should be cut up into small pieces and to this can be added a selection of diced vegetables in season. Carrots, onions, celery, turnips, all add a piquancy and flavour all of their own, and a light seasoning should be added before just covering with water.

This stew can either be cooked in a saucepan or in a casserole, but it needs to lightly simmer for two to three hours.

## BEEF STEAK PUDDING

To make the pastry for this you will need:

> 8 oz flour
> 4 oz suet
> Pinch of salt
> Water

Mix the ingredients into a stiff dough.

For the filling you will need:

> ¾ lb steak cut into thin pieces
> 6 oz ox kidney
> Half an onion, finely chopped
> Pepper and salt mixed with one tablespoonful of flour.

After you have greased the basin, line it with the pastry but save some for the covering. Add the ingredients in layers with the seasoning sprinkled between each layer. Three quarters fill with water and then cover with a pastry lid. Tie a cloth over the basin and steam for three-and-a-half hours.

## STEWED OXTAIL

You will need:

> 1 ox tail
> Sliced onions
> 2 oz butter
> Salt and pepper
> Bay leaf
> 1 tablespoonful of lemon juice
> 1½ oz flour
> 1 pint of stock or water

Wash and dry the ox tail and cut it into pieces. Heat the butter in the stewpan and then fry the pieces of ox tail in the butter until they are golden brown. Remove them and put in the sliced onions and flour. Fry until they are well browned and then add the stock, bay leaf, salt and pepper and stir until boiling. Replace the pieces of tail, cover tightly and simmer gently for 2½-3 hours.

Sutton Staithe
*Before they became sullied with sewage and cluttered with fibre-glass 'baths', the Broads and waterways of Norfolk provided home for countless smoothly rippling dinghies and for the great barges with their huge black sails; and those reeds—refuge for numerous small birds—thatch for the roofs of barns and cottages, a sea of green in summer, softly whispering, a cloud of brown in autumn, dryly rustling. Great stretches of clear clean water, with many a large pike rising, flowed gently through this lovely county to the sea.*

## COLD MEAT ROLLS

A delicious way to serve the remains of a joint of beef. Mince the cold beef and add some breadcrumbs—about half the bulk of the mince—with some finely chopped parsley, pepper and salt. Beat up one egg and stir into the mixture. Make some short crust pastry, roll out, and cut into about five inch squares. Fill the mixture on half the surface, double over the crust, pinching the edges together and then bake and serve hot.

If you would rather, you can add a little cold gravy or stock instead of the egg to moisten.

# Lamb

## LAMB CUTLETS

You will need:

    Mutton cutlets cut with two bones to each
    ¼ lb mushrooms
    1½ lbs shallots
    **Pepper and salt**
    **Butter**
    ½ pint stock

Take the cutlets and remove one bone from each. Flatten the cutlets and trim neatly and season. Cut them into two but do not divide at the bone. Cook the mushrooms, shallots and a little parsley in the butter and put a little of this inside each cutlet. Press the edges of the cutlet together and grill for about eight minutes. Mix some of the fried vegetables with the stock and heat gently. Pour this over the cutlets and they are ready for serving.

## BREAST OF MUTTON WITH CAPER SAUCE

You will need:

    1 breast of mutton
    2 tablespoonsful of breadcrumbs
    1 tablespoonful of suet
    1 dessertspoon of chopped parsley
    ½ teaspoonful of powdered mixed herbs
    Milk, salt and pepper
    ½ pint of caper sauce, stock or water
    1 onion
    1 carrot
    ½ small turnip
    10 peppercorns
    **Salt to taste**

Remove the bones and any superfluous fat from the breast of mutton, flatten the meat and season it well. Mix the breadcrumbs, suet, parsley, mixed herbs, pepper and salt together and moisten the mixture with milk. Spread the mixture on the meat, roll up lightly and bind up securely with string. Bring the caper sauce, or stock, to the boil, place the meat in it and simmer gently for two hours. Serve using the sauce, or stock, as gravy.

Chimney on fire
*An open fire is a wonderfully cheering thing in a room; on a cold winter's day its sight is as warming as its heat, but one of its drawbacks is the possibility of a chimney fire, often caused by an excess of soot in the chimney.*

*If your chimney catches fire, close all the doors leading into the room so that all upward draught may be stopped. Then throw some fine common salt on the fire in the grate, which will immediately extinguish that in the chimney.*

## KATHY'S STEW

    3 lb neck of mutton
    1 large onion
    1½ pints of stock
    4 lb potatoes
    12 button mushrooms
    Salt, pepper and a little chopped parsley.

Cut the meat into pieces and trim off some of the fat. Wash, peel, and slice the potatoes and the large onion. Peel the button mushrooms and blanch them. Put a layer of potatoes at the bottom of the stewpan, cover with a layer of meat, add a slice or two of onion and season well with salt and pepper. Repeat until all the ingredients are used, ensuring that the potatoes form the top layer. Between these layers, the button mushrooms should be interspersed. Add the stock and when it comes to the boil skim off any fat. Unless the meat is very fat, very little subsequent skimming is needed. The stewpan must be kept covered, and the contents cooked gently for about one-and-a-half hours, or until the potatoes are cooked and the stew loses its watery appearance.

Kathy the land girl
*Such a shame we never had a photograph of Kathy, the land girl who worked at Burnell's Farm, East Ruston, during the war. Lovely girl she was, with a smile as warm and fresh as the air in which she worked. Going down to South Fen with Kathy to get in Grandad's cows was always a summer day full of smiles and companionship— the most telling thing in childhood is a smile. She made a lovely stew and dumplings as well. Her recipe is here.*

# Dumplings

## NORFOLK DUMPLINGS

Light, fluffy and white are Norfolk dumplings; they are certainly not those monstrous diminutives to be found gasping for breath in stews. Simple, to make, requiring but a light hand and perseverance. You will need:

- ½ lb self-raising flour or ½ lb plain flour
- Pinch of salt
- 1 teaspoonful of baking powder
- Water to make a firm dough

Mix all the ingredients together to a medium dough. Separate into four portions and roll into balls. Steam for twenty minutes—no longer. They can either be put on top of the potatoes to cook or placed on top of soup. It is important to steam them.

## ONION DUMPLINGS

You will need:

- 8 oz self-raising flour
- 4 oz suet
- 4 oz finely chopped onion
- Salt and pepper
- Water or milk

Mix all the ingredients together and then add a little water or milk to make into a firm dough. Divide the mixture into small balls and roll them well in flour. Put the dumplings into soup or stew when it is simmering, about fifteen minutes before it has finished cooking. They should not be overcooked.

## BOILED BATTER PUDDING

Certainly different to Yorkshire pudding, this is a delicious dish which can either be used for a sweet, covered in treacle or jam when it is on the plate, or it can be used for accompanying savoury dishes. You will need:

- ¾ pint of milk
- 6 oz plain flour
- 3 eggs
- Pinch of salt

Mix the flour and salt together and make a well in the centre. Beat the eggs thoroughly, strain them into the flour and stir gently so that the flour gradually becomes incorporated. Add milk a little at a time until the batter has the consistency of thick cream, then cover and let it stand for at least one hour. When ready pour into a well-buttered basin, cover with a scalded, well-floured cloth and boil for about 1¼ hours.

# Salads

## SUMMER SALAD

Right in the middle of August when the heat hangs heavy in the sheltered garden and the crops there are at their most bountiful, pick and wash two lettuces. Take the large leaves at the base to line a large salad bowl. Take a head of endive, a cupful of fresh peas, a cupful of cooked potatoes, a few spring onions, two or three tomatoes and some fresh chopped herbs. Shred, chop and dice them all and blend them together with a little salad oil. Place them on the lettuce leaves in the salad bowl and garnish with a little cress. Aunty won't think much of it, but just see Uncle's eyes light up; especially when he sees the fresh salmon it is to accompany.

## WINTER SALAD

What . . . salad in winter? But fresh from the warmth of the fire and served with some slices of ham and tongue . . . winter salad . . . mmm, lovely. Take two apples, a quarter of an onion (more if you like it) and half a cooked beetroot. Cut them all up into small dice and toss them lightly in mayonnaise, or French dressing. In a little cut glass bowl with a little chopped parsely sprinkled on top it will turn a nutritious meal into an attractive one.

Lady at Cottage Door
*Round at the back of this cottage was a lovely garden where Mr. Spanton grew some lovely lettuce. In the shade of the old cottage, but warmed by the early morning sun, they grew as fresh and crisp as any we've ever had. And then at teatime, with the salad bowl on the table and our blue and white plates before us, what a lovely salad we'd have. The setting sun shone through the windows, bringing a soft rosy glow into the cool parlour.*

## SPRING SALAD

Mix a nice dressing of two tablespoonfuls of salad oil, salt, pepper and one tablespoonful of vinegar. Take the leaves off a lettuce and after they have been washed toss them in the salad dressing. Take two small leaves of white cabbage and shred finely after it has been washed. Cut six radishes and six spring onions and slice them thinly. Take the lettuce leaves and arrange them in the salad bowl and on top of them place the mixture of cabbage, onion and radish. Grate four carrots in the centre and pour a small drop of the salad dressing on it. Sprinkle with a little cress—and there you are—a lovely spring salad to accompany ham, chicken, or what you will.

## CROMER CRAB SALAD

In June or July there is no more delicious or succulent meal than this. Firstly go to Cromer and get a freshly cooked crab from one of the shops there. Dress it, as is explained on page 10, and take out all the meat and put it on a plate. Take six new potatoes which have been boiled and allowed to cool; dice them and mix them with the crab meat, adding a little mayonnaise to moisten it.

Lay a layer of lettuce leaves around the salad bowl and on top of this arrange some watercress. Lay thinly sliced tomatoes in a circle around the centre of the bowl and pile the crab and potato mixture on the top of this. Lovely.

## NEW POTATO SALAD

Go down the garden and dig a good root of new potatoes. Boil them lightly—mmm, delicious hot . . . and lovely cold in a salad. Take some new potatoes which have been boiled and allowed to cool and slice them thinly. Mix with cold peas, parsley and a little tarragon. Arrange this in a bowl and add some sliced hard-boiled egg. A little lettuce and tomato on a side plate . . . wowee—scrumptious.

Remedy for flies on horses
Extracted from an old book written by someone in the 1860's in a fine copperplate writing:
"An excellent remedy for flies: Take two or three handfuls of walnut leaves, upon which pour two or three quarts of cold water; let them infuse one night, and pour the whole next morning into a kettle, and let them boil for a quarter of an hour. When cold the mixture is fit for use. Before the horse goes out of the stable moisten a sponge and let those parts which are most irritable be smeared over with the liquor."

# HAM SALAD

For the best results you need one of those large hams which have been salted and smoked and left to hang on the kitchen hook for a winter, but if you can't do this, take a quarter of a pound of the best ham you can buy and cut it into neat dice. Dice one beetroot and thinly slice a few spring onions. Take a good lettuce and arrange the best leaves around the inside of a salad bowl. Shred the rest of the lettuce and add it to the ham, beetroot, spring onions and blend them together with a little mayonnaise. Place this mixture on to the lettuce leaves in the salad bowl and garnish with sliced tomatoes. Bootiful.

# STUFFED JACKET POTATOES

To warm up a salad for winter, take;

>    6 medium sized baked jacket potatoes
>    2 tablespoonsful of butter
>    2 beaten whites of eggs
>    3 tablespoonfuls of hot milk
>    Seasoning

When the potatoes have baked, slice each lengthways and scoop out the inside. Mash, add butter, salt, pepper and hot milk. Mix well and then stir in frothed whites of eggs. Stuff this into the potato jackets, and if you like, sprinkle with grated cheese. Bake them for a further five to eight minutes in a very hot oven.

To dry herbs
*Herbs should be gathered on a dry day at the time when the plant is about to flower. The root should be cut off and the plant washed if necessary. On a warm bright day, spread the leaves out and allow them to dry until they are crisp but not brown. The leaves should be rubbed through a coarse sieve before being bottled in airtight containers.*

# Pickles

## PICCALILLI

Cut up two pounds each of cauliflower, shallots and onions. Sprinkle with a little salt and allow to stand for twenty-four hours.

Boil together two quarts of vinegar, a few chillies and one ounce of turmeric powder. Wash the vegetables and put them into the vinegar mixture and boil for ten minutes. Mix together four ounces of mustard and one tablespoonful of flour with a little cold vinegar. Add this to the vegetable mixture and boil for two minutes longer.

Allow to cool and then bottle.

## PICKLED ONIONS

Choose small pickling onions or shallots. Peel them carefully without cutting the onion. Wash them and cover them with brine which is made by mixing sufficient water to cover the onions and two ounces of salt to each pint of water needed. Allow the onions to stand in this brine for twenty four hours.

Drain them, wash and dry before packing the onions into jars. Cover the onions with cold spiced vinegar and seal the top.

## MARROW CHUTNEY

Cut up a three pound marrow and place it in a basin. Sprinkle the pieces with two teaspoonfuls of salt and leave for about twenty-four hours. After that the marrow should be drained and rinsed. Take half-a-pound of green apples, and half-a-pound of shallots and chop them very finely. Tie 12 peppercorns and a ¼ oz bruised ginger in a muslin bag.

Put into the saucepan 1¼ pints of vinegar, the marrow, the chopped shallots and apples, half-a-pound of sultanas and allow the muslin bag of herbs to float in the vinegar. Bring to the boil slowly and allow to simmer for one or two hours until it is of the correct consistency. Stir occasionally to prevent burning.

When it is cooked, remove the muslin bag, then put the mixture at once into hot, sterilised jars and cover immediately.

Norwich Provision Market
*The ancient Norwich market was a fascinating place. You never knew what you might find around the corner. A variety of individual characters and wares could be found, and not only were they interesting, but they all had something of value and worth too. And today, even though the stalls are regimented, the individuality of the Norfolk people smiles through.*

# Puddings

## SUMMER PUDDING

You will need:

    8 oz bread without the crust, cut into thin slices
    1½ lb fresh hot stewed fruit
    4—6 ozs sugar to taste
    A little water

Line a greased basin with bread. Pour in a good bit of the fruit and then lay across another slice of bread. Add some more fruit and then another piece of bread and so on until the basin is full. The last layer should be a slice of bread. Put a weighted plate on the top. Turn out carefully when it is cold. Can be served with custard.

## EAST RUSTON DELIGHT

A lovely light pudding:
You will need:

    ½ lb flour
    1 egg
    2 oz sugar
    3 oz suet
    1 teaspoon of bicarbonate of soda
    2 tablespoonsful of strawberry jam
    1 dessertspoonful of milk

Mix the dry ingredients together thoroughly, add the jam, beat up the egg and stir in. Dissolve the bicarbonate of soda in the milk and add last. Only fill the basin a little over half for this pudding will rise very much. Steam for 2½ hours.

Headaches
*This painful affliction brought on by tension and stress is ill served by those chemical tablets abounding in bottle and box. Better by far to use nature's remedies which do not tear at the layer of the stomach. A little nutmeg, grated into a mug of boiling water, inhaled rather than drunk, often brings welcome relief. Some say that a thimbleful of whisky rubbed sharply in the hands and held to the nose cures headache at one; however, in most of our lives whisky is the cause rather than the cure for headache. Camomile tea is a well-known curative; lesser known is the lavender, the scent of which lessens the tension.*

**Cottages**
*These trim little clay lump and thatched cottages at East Ruston have now sadly gone; in their place a crude bungalow. This has been the trend for the past thirty or forty years, but, if well cared for, these roofs and walls would have stood warm and sound for many, many years. Strange how some peoples idea of progress is to remove the characteristics of places, be it in dialect, customs, recipes, houses or clothes, and replace them with characterless nonentities.*

## QUEEN'S PUDDING

You will need:

    1 pint milk
    1 oz castor sugar
    ½ pint breadcrumbs
    ¾ oz butter
    Grated rind of 1 lemon
    2 eggs
    Jam

Boil the milk and pour over the breadcrumbs. Add the sugar, butter, lemon rind and, when it has cooled a little, stir in the beaten yolks of eggs. Place the mixture in a buttered pie dish and bake at a medium temperature for ten minutes, or until it has set. Now spread on a thick layer of jam and cover with the stiffly beaten whites of egg. Dredge well with the castor sugar. Return it to the oven and bake until the meringue hardens and acquires a little colour—about one hour.

## BLACK CAP PUDDING

You will need:

    4 oz self-raising flour
    ½ pint milk
    1 oz sugar
    1 egg
    1 oz currants
    1 good pinch of salt

Put the flour and the salt into a basin. Make a well in the centre and break in the egg. Add the milk a little at a time and stir gradually, working in the flour. When about half the milk has been used, give the batter a good beating. Then add the rest of the milk, and sugar, and currants. Place the mixture in a pudding basin and it may be cooked at once, but it will lighten a great deal if it is first allowed to stand for one hour. Cover with a greased paper. The pudding should be steamed for one hour.

The friend of man
*Dog is the friend of man and has a right to be considered as such. He has an expression in the eye that can be found in no other but the human being; like man he can look grave or show delight. His power to plead is by a strangely expressive look, and his power of love shows itself in delight.*

# GOLDEN PUDDING

You will need:

    8 oz self-raising flour
    5 oz raisins
    1 gill of milk
    2 oz breadcrumbs
    5 oz margarine
    1 egg
    2 tablespoonsful of syrup
    1 teaspoonful of ground ginger

Mix all the dry ingredients together and then melt the syrup and add this and the milk, and then the egg. Really mix them together well. Pour the mixture into a basin which has been lined with butter and cover with greaseproof paper or a pudding cloth. Boil for two-and-a-half hours or more.

The pudding bowl

*I wonder where the child is who will certainly want to clean out the bowl afterwards? That doesn't alter as the years go by, and you don't have to be a child to think that the cake and pudding mixture tastes better "raw".*

*It doesn't take long to bake, so why bother with shop bought cakes and puddings? Why deprive a child of the uncooked mixture?*

## GINGER PUDDING

You will need:

      6 oz self-raising flour
      1 small teaspoon of ground ginger
      a pinch of salt
      2 tablespoonsful of syrup
      1 egg
      2 oz shredded suet, or margarine
      2 oz crystallised ginger
      ½ pint milk

Mix the suet and all the dry ingredients. Beat the egg and add this together with the syrup and the milk. Well stir the whole mixture. Put a tablespoonful of syrup in a greased basin, pour in the mixture and steam (or boil) for two hours.

Serve with sweet sauce or golden syrup.

Old Norwich, from river
*The bridge from which this picture was taken in 1905 still stands at the beginning of Magdalen Street. The River Wensum was a busy highway for barges and other river traffic. Timber is being unloaded here, but that was just one of the many commodities that passed this way. The silent windows of the workplaces and warehouses stare grimly into our world of the 1980's.*

# Cakes & Buns

## NORFOLK RASPBERRY BUNS

You will need:

    6 oz ground rice
    6 oz lard
    A pinch of baking powder
    4 oz self-raising flour
    4 oz sugar
    2 beaten eggs

Rub the lard into the flour, add the other dry ingredients and beat into a stiff paste with the egg, but leaving a little beaten egg for glazing the buns. Divide into little balls and put a little raspberry jam in each and close up again. Brush with the remaining egg and bake quickly in a hot oven, about 425°. When they are cracked and showing jam they are sufficiently baked.

## HARRY BROKE CAKE

You will need:

    ¾ lb self-raising flour
    ½ lb sugar
    ½ lb butter
    1 lb mixed fruit
    3 or 4 eggs

Mix sugar and flour well and then add the butter, followed by the eggs which should have been well beaten. When it is formed into a nice stiff paste, add the fruit and mix well. Put into a greased cake tin and bake for 1½ to 2 hours in an oven at 350°.

### Sleep

*It has been said that one hour's sleep before midnight is worth three after, and that five minutes' sleep is equal to one pound of beefsteak. One of the best ways to ensure a good night's sleep is to use a hop pillow. In certain places in the Norfolk lanes and byways are to be found the fronds of wild hops. Gather the hops in the autumn and dry them gently in the last warm sunshine of the year. A few dried leaves of ladies mantle add to the relaxing fragrance.*

## SURPRISE CAKES

You will need:

    4 oz margarine
    2 eggs
    8 oz flour
    pinch of salt
    4 oz castor sugar
    Glazed cherries
    Jam

Beat the eggs in a basin, warm the margarine add to the eggs and beat again. Mix together the flour, salt and the sugar and gradually add this to the eggs and margarine, beating all the time. Grease some small bun tins, and put a little of the mixture at the bottom of each. Then, in the middle, put half a teaspoon of jam. Cover with more of the cake mixture. Put a glace cherry on the top of each and bake in an over of about 400°–425° until golden brown.

## HARVEST FOURSES CAKE

You will need:

    6 oz self-raising flour
    2 oz chopped crystallised ginger
    3 oz castor sugar
    2 oz margarine
    1 egg

Mix the margarine and sugar together and beat into a cream. Add the eggs, mix in the flour and ginger and beat well. The mixture should be placed in small tins or baking cases and the top sprinkled with sugar. They should be baked for about twenty minutes in an oven at 400°.

## SHORT CAKES

You will need:

    6 oz flour
    6 oz currants
    6 oz butter
    4 oz castor sugar
    2 oz ground rice
    Yolk of one egg
    A pinch of salt

Preheat the oven to 375°. Mix together the flour, ground rice and salt. Rub in the butter then add the sugar and currants and mix together. Add the yolk of the egg and mix it all together to make a smooth dough. Roll out flat until it is half-an-inch thick, and either cut it into squares of about three inches, or into circles with a wine-glass. Put in oven for about twenty minutes.

Strange

*Mothers lean to sons, fathers to daughters. Also, before the birth of a child, the mother is anxious to know its sex, and this may be known thus—if the previous child born had peaked hair in the neck it will be a boy, but if straight hair, it will be a girl.*

**Having tea at Great Yarmouth**
*"Delicious cakes aren't they, my dear? And these lovely cups, so delicate, they make this tea taste even more refreshing. No, John was in this hammock a minute ago, I wonder where he's gone? Mmmm, my dear, don't they treat us well; we'll have to come again. Wonder what Arthur's up to . . . I hope he's behaving himself . . . I didn't like the look that that girl selling ice-creams gave him. He would you know."*

## OLD TIMES GINGERBREAD

You will need:

    1 lb self-raising flour
    4 oz sugar
    ¾ oz ground ginger
    ½ teaspoon of carbonate of soda
    4 tablespoonsful of golden syrup
    6 oz margarine
    2 oz almonds
    2 oz candied peel
    1 teaspoon of mixed spice
    1 egg

Cut the almonds and candied peel and mix them well with the ginger, spice and flour. Slightly warm the syrup and add to the margarine, and sugar; beat this to a cream. Add the egg. Dissolve the soda in a little milk. Now mix all the ingredients together and mix them well. Bake in an oven at about 325° for two hours, being careful not to shake it.

## MARROW CUSTARD

A favourite recipe of childhood memory.

Boil a marrow for about twenty minutes until it is soft. Meanwhile, make an egg custard from two eggs, 1 oz sugar and one pint of milk, all of which should be beaten well together. Make a small piece of pastry and line a pie dish with it.

When the marrow has cooked, strain it and mash it up well with a fork. Put it into a large basin and pour the egg custard over the top of it. Stir it all up. If you wish, add a little more sugar. Pour the custard and marrow into the pastry lined dish and grate a little nutmeg over the top of it.

Put it into an oven of 250° and bake for 30—45 minutes. It is delicious served either hot or cold.

## BRANCASTER TART

You will need:

    8 oz shortcrust pastry, chilled
    ½ lb golden syrup
    1 oz butter
    2 small eggs, well beaten
    2 tblspns black treacle
    little grated lemon rind
    3 tblspns cream, or evaporated milk

An old dear in Brancaster could tempt anyone into her house by offering her special treacle tart! It's easy to make too.

Roll out the pastry and line an 8 inch flan ring. Place a circle of greaseproof paper on top of this and sprinkle rice on it to keep it from rising. Bake in a moderate oven for 15 minutes then remove the paper and rice. This is called 'Baking Blind'. Gently warm the syrup and the black treacle then remove from heat. Add the butter, in small pieces, and when it is all melted add the rest of the ingredients. Mix this thoroughly and poor it into the pastry case.

Cook in middle of oven, at moderate temperature, and continue cooking, until the filling is set. It will only take 15 or 20 minutes and I bet you will want to eat some before it even cools down properly!

**Harvest picture**
*Loose barley being gathered in and loaded on to the tumbrils to be stacked. Great barley forks were used and these can be seen in old farm museums. Lovely to look back on but loading barley was an awful job for pitcher and stacker alike. The barley hands went down your neck, up your trousers and everywhere. On hot days with sweat trickling down it was a thirsty and hungry job. Mind you, when the tea and cakes were brought at four o'clock and you sat down on a pile of straw it seemed all worth it. Tea has never tasted as good as it did from that large jug, poured into large cups . . . and the cakes, crumbly, warm and delicious.*

# Drinks

Once, when cutting a hedge with a hook and stick, in the blazing heat of a still, Norfolk August, I happened to be near the cottage of one of those lovely little old white-haired ladies. A soul of innocence smiled out of her face as she stood in the doorway of her little quiet cottage. "Would you like a drop of wine? You look very hot." she cooed. "Be all right." I responded . . . who was innocent now? Out she came with her rhubarb wine. "And another drop?" when the first was done. Five glasses I had . . . a hot sunny day. Beggar the old hedge.

Mind you, when I went round that autumn, we enjoyed a lovely glass of damson wine. I held it up to the lamp light—an old oil lamp on the table-cloth—sunshine streamed through the ruby wine. Autumn . . . soft lamp light . . . and damson wine. The air was velvet as I walked home.

## DAMSON WINE

Gather the fruit, dry, weigh it and bruise it, and to every eight pounds of fruit add one gallon of water. Boil the water and pour it on the fruit scalding hot. Let it stand for two days.

Then draw it off and put it into a clean cask; to every gallon of liquor add two and a half pounds of sugar. Fill the cask.

It may be bottled off after standing in the cask for a year. On bottling the wine put a small lump of sugar into every bottle.

## NORFOLK COTTAGE CIDER

12lbs apples
1 gallon warm water
Yeast — optional
1 lb raisins, chopped
1½-2lbs sugar

After washing, put the apples through a mincer, or chop them very, very finely, and place them in a polythene bucket. Add the water, raisins, sugar and yeast if you intend to use it. Some people can make this cider successfully without yeast. Stir the mixture well and cover. Leave the bucket in a warm place for 2 weeks, but stir and push the pulp down every day. Strain the liquid, through muslin, into a fermentation jar, squeezing the pulp gently to extract all of the juice. Insert an airlock and allow to ferment right out. Then the jar needs to be kept in a cooler place for a month. After this time syphon the cider into strong bottles and tie the corks down.

This can be drunk whenever you like, but the longer you leave it, the better, and the stronger, it will be!

### Herbs
*It is best to raise parsley and fennel from seed. Tansy, rue, sage and rosemary can best be grown from cutting slips. Basil, thyme, marjoram and balm are best developed from dividing roots. Fennel, dill and basil should be sown in May, and other herbs should be sown in March.*

Motor cycle and sidecar
*John, did you hear. Tell that boy to come off that motor bike. You never know what he's going to touch, and me sitting here in this thing. You know I don't like it. John, did you hear? Now Reggie get off that . . . he's taken the photograph now. We'll go to Dolcis for a lovely ham salad and if you're good we'll get you an ice-cream. Reggie, did you hear? Perhaps what she really needs is a stiff drink!*

## NORFOLK PUNCH

You will need:

    1 pint of good brandy
    1½ pints of well water or spring water
    1 small egg white
    1 small Seville orange
    1 small lemon
    7 oz castor sugar

Peel the orange and the lemon very thinly and cut the rind into small pieces before putting them into the brandy. Allow it to stand for at least four days so that the brandy may absorb all the flavour from the rind.

Pour the spring or well water into a saucepan and add the egg white and the castor sugar. Boil this for half-an-hour, occasionally skimming any scum from the surface. Allow it to cool then remove the peel.

When it is cool pour the brandy into it, and squeeze in the juice of the lemon and orange. It should then be placed in a pot, covered with muslin and allowed to stand for at least six weeks.

The punch should then be filtered, or poured off, to leave the sediment, and bottled until required.

## SLOE WINE

Marvellous if you can make it.

    1 gallon of ripe sloes
    4 lb sugar
    1 gallon of boiling water

Pick the sloes when they are ripe and place them in a bowl. After you have rinsed and drained them, pour the boiling water over them and allow to stand for one week, stirring them first thing in the morning and last thing at night. Strain out the sloes after a week and stir in the sugar. When it is dissolved put it into bottles or a cask to work. When the working is finished, cork down loosely at first, then tighten the corks after a day or two.

## RASPBERRY WINE

Bruise the fruit and put the juice into a cask. Bung it closed for forty-eight hours, after which open the bung for two days. Replace the bung after forty-eight hours and let it stand for three months before bottling.

The longer a wine stands, the richer it grows.

# SYLLABUB

You will need:

    1 pint of milk
    ½ pint of cider
    8 oz castor sugar
    1 wineglass of light white wine
    1 nutmeg and 1 lemon

Place the cider, the white wine, the sugar and the juice from the lemon in a bowl and stir to mix. Warm the milk and place it in a teapot and pour over the cider mixture from arm held quite high. Grate in a little nutmeg. Whisk until it is thickened and then pour into glasses and chill for several hours before serving.

To clean wine decanters
*Soak the decanters (or vinegar and sauce cruets) in soda and warm water. If there is much cutting on the outside a brush will be necessary to remove the dirt and stains from the crevices. Cut a potato into small dice, put in a good handful of these with some warm water; shake the decanter briskly until the stains disappear, rinse in cold water and let them drain dry.*

## JUST LIKE HIS MOTHER
## USED TO DO

Our George got marrid wun foin day,
Tu his choildhood sweethart Sue,
He thowt thet she'd look arter him
Just loike his mother useter dew.

They went on honimoon ter Clact'n,
And hed a luv'ly weekind fer two
But he wuz gled to git hoom agin
Just loike his mother useter dew.

Fer Sundi dinna, yung Sue arst him
Wot he'd loike har tu dew,
"O sum gud roost beef end luv'li grearvy
Just loike moy mother useter dew."

When he cum in frum the gardin,
He sed ter let the teepot brew,
On the kitch'n rairnge for a whoile
Just loike his mother useter dew.

On Mundi he arst har furra tea
Uv 'taters and rich beef stew,
And he towld good Sue ter cook't
Just loike his mother useter dew.

But she meard him a jinja pudden,
She thowt he'd injoy suffin new,
But thet wuz tarned asoide fur thet woont cook't
Just loike his mother useter dew.

When he left har luv'ly pudden,
Har anga jest grew 'n grew
An' she give him a good hard clip o' thu lug
Jest loike his mother useter dew.

"Now yew look heer," she towld him,
"I're hed unuff o' yew.
Yew eet thet jinja pudden up,
Jest loike oime a'tellin' yew tew."

An' George . . . ? . . . he smoiled an' sed
"Ah, good ole Sue, yew'll dew,
Oime gled yew spook ter me loike thet
Thass jest loike mother useter dew."

# Cures & Preventatives

**To give a cat some medicine**
When a favourite cat requires medicine from having eaten some sort of refuse, simply dip its foot in castor oil, which it is sure to lick.

**To prevent attacks from gnats**
The best preventive against gnats, as well as the best cure for their stings, is camphor.

To make some camphor ice, mix one ounce of spermaceti, a quarter of an ounce of white wax, and half-an-ounce of camphor, in one ounce of olive oil. Put these ingredients into an earthenware jar; set it in a cool oven and while melting stir frequently. Pour into little pots for use.

**To prevent the ravages of insects on trees and flowers**
For those who deplore the use of insecticides in this conservation age, take a tip from an old gardener. Mix nine parts of water with one part of French vinegar and sprinkle the mixture over the flower beds by means of a watering pot, or syringe with a fine rose.

**Simple cure for a wasp sting**
A slice of common onion rubbed on the sting, or if in the throat, chewed slowly and the pieces swallowed, is a certain cure. Many years ago a poor woman was stung in the throat by swallowing a wasp in some beer. She at once ate an onion and the swelling was checked directly and the pain afterwards soon abated.

# INDEX

BEEF—
- Beef Steak Pudding ... 20
- Beef Stew ... 20
- Cold Meat Rolls ... 21
- Oxtail, stewed ... 20

CAKES AND BUNS—
- Brancaster Tart ... 38
- Harry Broke Cake ... 35
- Harvest Fourses Cake ... 36
- Marrow Custard ... 38
- Norfolk Raspberry Buns ... 35
- Old Times Gingerbread ... 38
- Short Cakes ... 36
- Surprise Cakes ... 36

DRINKS—
- Damson Wine ... 40
- Norfolk Cottage Cider ... 40
- Norfolk Punch ... 42
- Raspberry Wine ... 42
- Sloe Wine ... 42
- Syllabub ... 43

DUMPLINGS—
- Boiled Batter Pudding ... 24
- Norfolk Dumplings ... 24
- Onion Dumplings ... 24

FISH—
- Bloaters and Kippers ... 12
- Dressed Crab ... 10
- Kedgeree ... 12
- Soused Herrings ... 10
- Stookey Blues ... 12

LAMB—
- Breast of Mutton with Caper Sauce ... 22
- Kathy's Stew ... 23
- Lamb Cutlets ... 22

PICKLES—
- Marrow Chutney ... 28
- Piccalilli ... 28
- Pickled onions ... 28

PORK—
- Pork and Marrow Pie ... 15
- Pork and Onion Dumpling ... 15
- Pork Cheese ... 14

POULTRY AND GAME—
- Cockerel roast ... 16
- Duck, roast wild duck with orange salad ... 17
- Goose, Christmas Goose Pie ... 17
- Hare, Jugged ... 18
- Pheasant, Roast ... 18
- Rabbit pie ... 19
- Turkey Cheese ... 16

PUDDINGS—
- Black Cap Pudding ... 32
- East Ruston Delight ... 30
- Ginger Pudding ... 34
- Golden Pudding ... 33
- Queen's Pudding ... 32
- Summer Pudding ... 30

SALADS—
- Cromer Crab Salad ... 25
- Ham Salad ... 27
- New Potato Salad ... 26
- Spring Salad ... 25
- Stuffed Jacket Potatoes ... 27
- Summer Salad ... 26
- Winter Salad ... 26

SOUPS—
- Asparagus Soup ... 9
- Kidney Soup ... 8
- Onion Soup ... 8
- Pea Soup ... 7